Next Generation
ENERGY

FRACKING

Fracturing Rock to Reach Oil and Gas Underground

Nancy Dickmann

CRABTREE
Publishing Company
www.crabtreebooks.com

Crabtree Publishing Company
www.crabtreebooks.com

Author: Nancy Dickmann

Editors: Sarah Eason, Jen Sanderson, and Shirley Duke

Proofreader: Katie Dicker and Wendy Scavuzzo

Editorial director: Kathy Middleton

Design: Paul Myerscough and Geoff Ward

Cover design: Paul Myerscough

Photo research: Sarah Eason and Jen Sanderson

Prepress technician: Margaret Amy Salter

Print coordinator: Margaret Amy Salter

Consultant: Richard Spilsbury, degree in Zoology, 30 years as an author and editor of educational science books

Written and produced for Crabtree Publishing by Calcium Creative

Library and Archives Canada Cataloguing in Publication

Dickmann, Nancy, author
      Fracking : fracturing rock to reach oil and gas underground / Nancy Dickmann.

(Next generation energy)
Includes index.
Issued in print and electronic formats.
ISBN 978-0-7787-1984-7 (bound).--
ISBN 978-0-7787-2007-2 (paperback).--
ISBN 978-1-4271-1642-0 (pdf).--
ISBN 978-1-4271-1634-5 (html)

      1. Hydraulic fracturing--Juvenile literature. 2. Hydraulic fracturing--Environmental aspects--Juvenile literature. 3. Gas well drilling--Juvenile literature. 4. Gas well drilling--Environmental aspects--Juvenile literature. I. Title.

TN880.2.D53 2015   j622'.3381   C2015-903224-5
                                               C2015-903225-3

Library of Congress Cataloging-in-Publication Data

Dickmann, Nancy.
 Fracking : fracturing rock to reach oil and gas underground / Nancy Dickmann.
      pages cm. -- (Next generation energy)
 Includes index.
 ISBN 978-0-7787-1984-7 (reinforced library binding : alk. paper) --
ISBN 978-0-7787-2007-2 (pbk. : alk. paper) --
ISBN 978-1-4271-1642-0 (electronic pdf : alk. paper) --
ISBN 978-1-4271-1634-5 (electronic html : alk. paper)
 1. Hydraulic fracturing--Juvenile literature. I. Title.

TN871.255D53 2015
622'.3381--dc23

                    2015022003

Crabtree Publishing Company
www.crabtreebooks.com   1-800-387-7650

Printed in Canada/082015/BF20150630

Published in Canada
Crabtree Publishing
616 Welland Ave.
St. Catharines, Ontario
L2M 5V6

Published in the United States
Crabtree Publishing
PMB 59051
350 Fifth Avenue, 59th Floor
New York, New York 10118

Published in the United Kingdom
Crabtree Publishing
Maritime House
Basin Road North, Hove
BN41 1WR

Published in Australia
Crabtree Publishing
3 Charles Street
Coburg North
VIC, 3058

Contents

What Is Energy?

Energy is the ability to do work. It comes in many forms, such as electrical energy and chemical energy. We get a lot of our energy from fuels such as oil and coal. We rely on this energy to heat our homes, cook our food, and power our vehicles and factories. As the world's population grows, our need for energy increases.

There are many different ways of generating power and they all have disadvantages as well as advantages. Some types of power, such as tidal power, are difficult and expensive to **extract**. Other fuels, such as natural gas and coal, release **greenhouse gases** when they are burned. These gases rise into Earth's **atmosphere**, where they cause the planet's temperature to rise. This **climate change** has a serious impact on Earth's **climate**, and it is one of the most serious problems facing the world today. Even cleaner forms of power such as wind and solar, which do not release greenhouse gases, are expensive to set up and can only be used in certain places.

Huge amounts of energy and natural resources power the factories that produce the goods we use every day.

A Changing World

The past decades have seen many changes in the sources of energy people use. The use of **renewable** energy technologies, such as wind power and hydroelectric power, has increased. Improved technology has made them cheaper and more **efficient**. In the meantime, disasters such as the Deepwater Horizon oil spill in 2010 and the Fukushima nuclear disaster in 2011 have shaken people's confidence in some other forms of energy. Engineers are always looking for better—and cleaner—ways to power the world. In the last ten years, the energy landscape has been transformed by a new technology: fracking.

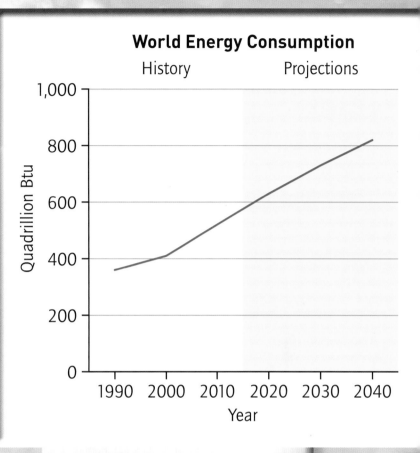

This graph shows how worldwide energy consumption has increased in recent years and it includes estimates of future needs.

The Energy Future: You Choose

Choosing which type of energy to use can be a balancing act. Cleaner fuels are often more expensive, and in many places, they are not available. Environmental concerns, such as **pollution** and **sustainability**, have to be weighed against cost, availability, and other factors. What do you think are the most important things to consider when choosing what type of fuel to use? Give reasons for your answer.

Fracking Basics

Deep beneath Earth's surface are vast reserves of oil and natural gas. For more than 150 years, people have been drilling down to reach these fuels. They are called fossil fuels, because they are made from the remains of organisms that lived millions of years ago. New supplies of fossil fuels take millions of years to form, so we will eventually run out of them.

A traditional deposit of oil or gas is usually found in a pocket between layers of different types of rocks in Earth's crust. A well is drilled down to the pocket, allowing the gas or oil to travel up the **borehole** to be collected. This is a relatively straightforward job and over the decades, engineers have greatly improved the technique. However, there are many other deposits where the fossil fuels are locked in the rock itself, trapped as tiny bubbles within the structure of the rock. These fuels are nearly impossible to extract in the traditional way.

water well

oil well

gas

oil

water

In this diagram, you can see how Earth's crust is arranged in layers of different types of rocks. Water, oil, and natural gas are often trapped between these layers.

A New idea

Fracking has been in the news a lot recently, but what exactly is it? It is not a new type of fuel or a new way of generating electricity. It is the word usually used for a process called hydraulic fracturing, or hydrofracking. It is a technique for reaching fossil fuels that were previously too hard to get to because they were trapped in layers of **shale** rock. Engineers have known about these deposits for a long time, but it was only fairly recently that they developed fracking as a new technology to extract them. Fracking is done by forcing liquid at extremely high **pressure** into the rock. The liquid breaks up, or fractures the rock, releasing the natural gas or oil.

A lot of the technology used in fracking is based on technology for traditional oil and natural gas drilling.

FAST FORWARD

Natural gas is widely used for heating, cooking, and fueling power stations, but it is not yet a popular fuel for cars. The use of fracking is increasing the supply of natural gas and making it cheaper. If people started using it in their cars, it could lead to cheaper and cleaner transportation. However, would it be better in the long run to look at other methods of transportation that could reduce our reliance on cars and fuel to run them? What would be the possible effects on the environment? Explain your thinking.

Fracking Products

Fracking can be used to extract different types of oil and gas. These are often called unconventional fuels because they are extracted using methods other than conventional drilling. The end products can be used in the same way as any other oil or natural gas, once they are extracted and refined.

Shale gas is the most common fuel to be extracted by fracking. It consists of tiny amounts of natural gas trapped in shale rock, a little like the small pockets of air in a loaf of bread. In 2000, it provided only 1 percent of the natural gas produced in the United States. By 2013, that figure had risen to more than 35 percent. The Energy Information Administration (EIA) estimates that by 2035, shale gas will make up 46 percent of the natural gas extracted in the United States.

Another type of unconventional fuel is tight gas, which is trapped in deposits of silt or sand. Shale oil is too thick and heavy to be extracted using conventional methods. It contains high amounts of sulfur and metals, which make it harder to pump and refine. Tar sands (sometimes called "oil sands") are deposits of heavy oil that is too thick to flow. It can be extracted only by pumping hot steam into the deposit.

Coal is a type of solid fossil fuel that is much easier to extract than unconventional fuels. Huge mines can tap into deposits near the surface.

Unconventional and Unpopular?

In general, unconventional fuels are more difficult to reach and more expensive to produce than regular fossil fuels. Extracting them is also usually more damaging to the **environment**. However, the demand for energy is increasing, and traditional oil reserves are being used up. Combined with improved fracking technology, this has led to more use of unconventional fuels such as shale oil and shale gas. Fracking for unconventional fuels has also made the United States less dependent on other countries for its energy needs.

Canada has some of the world's largest deposits of tar sands, and their oil industry produces more than 1 million barrels of oil a day from these resources.

REWIND

When people first started to use nuclear power in the 1950s, it was very controversial. The technology had first been used for nuclear bombs, and people were worried about the possible dangers. However, the cleanliness and efficiency of nuclear power eventually won over at least some of its critics. Fracking is as controversial now as nuclear power once was. Could people's opinions about fracking change, too, or do they even need to change their opinion?

The Dawn of Fracking

People have known about natural gas for centuries, although in the distant past they did not understand what it was. Sometimes, lightning would ignite natural gas that was escaping from the ground, creating fires that could last a long time. Many people thought that gods or monsters had caused these fires.

Centuries later, in 1859, Edwin Drake dug the first well in the United States, hitting oil and natural gas at 69 feet (21 m) below the surface. He built a **pipeline** to take the natural gas to a nearby village. Like Drake's well, most wells were dug straight down into **porous** limestone or sandstone formations. These are called **vertical** wells.

This early oil district was set up in Los Angeles, California, more than 100 years ago.

The administration of President Carter (1977–81) prioritized the development of new sources of energy, including unconventional fuels.

New Techniques

In the 1860s, some **prospectors** used an **explosive** called nitroglycerin to fracture oil wells. The technique was dangerous and illegal, but it worked. Later, it was used in water and gas wells. However, it was not until the 1940s that the first serious experiments with fracking took place. An engineer named Floyd Farris showed that using high-pressure fluid could get more oil and gas out of traditional wells. The process was **patented** in 1949.

Research into new technologies continued through the 1970s and 1980s. The studies were often supported by the United States government, especially during the energy crisis of 1973. In the 1980s, George P. Mitchell successfully worked oil and gas fields in Texas that other drillers had given up on, but the cost of extracting the gas was still too high to compete with other fuels. By the late 1990s, he had improved the technology and brought down the costs. Shale gas had become an affordable alternative to conventional gas.

REWIND

In the early days of oil and as drilling, energy companies were not required to protect the environment in the same way they are today. This was partly because no one realized how much harm they sometimes caused. Now, there are strict regulations on where and how companies can drill, but these rules can reduce production or make it more expensive. Do you think these regulations are a good thing? Explain your reasons.

How It Works

The term "fracking" usually refers to two techniques that are often used together. One is horizontal drilling, in which holes are bored horizontally across a shale formation. The other is hydraulic fracturing, in which high-pressure fluids are used to crack open the rock and allow gas to escape.

The first step in the fracking process is to drill a vertical well into the shale, which is usually more than 0.5 mile (0.8 km) below the surface. Once the shale is reached, the drill is turned sideways and it then continues to drill horizontally through the rock. The horizontal part of a fracked well can reach for another 2 miles (3.2 km).

When the drilling is finished, the entire borehole is lined with a steel casing. This casing keeps the gas from escaping and protects the surrounding ground from pollution. Next, thousands of tiny holes are made in the horizontal section of the steel casing. This is usually done by **detonating**, or exploding, a set of small, aimed charges inside the pipe.

Horizontal drilling is also called directional drilling. It allows energy companies to reach a wider, more spread out layer of shale gas.

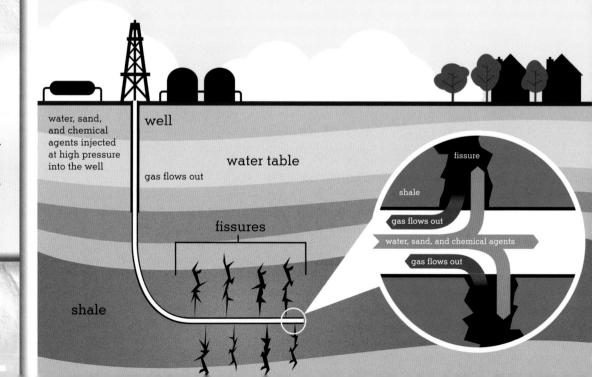

water, sand, and chemical agents injected at high pressure into the well

well

gas flows out

water table

fissures

shale

fissure

shale

gas flows out

water, sand, and chemical agents

gas flows out

Time to Frack

A mixture of water, sand, and chemicals is pumped into the well at very high pressure. When this fluid escapes through the tiny holes in the well casing, it fractures the rock where gas is trapped. Tiny pieces of sand and other solid material in the fracking fluid help to hold open the fractures, allowing the gas to flow out of the rock and up the pipe.

In the flowback phase, the pressure is reduced, and the fracking fluid comes back up to the surface. This **wastewater** has to be disposed of safely. Sometimes, it is injected into underground storage wells, or recycled to use in other fracked wells. Some of the wastewater is spread on roads or fields.

Fracking companies often create ponds near their operations, either to store fresh water before it is used, or for storing wastewater until it can be treated.

FAST FORWARD

One of the most controversial aspects of fracking is the amount of water it uses: a single well can use more than 10 million gallons (39 million liters) before it is fully operational. Some engineers are working on different materials to use instead of water. Others are developing more effective ways of treating the wastewater. Do you think these improvements will make fracking more appealing? Could the wastewater enter the environment safely if it is not treated?

Where in the World?

Oil and gas reserves are not spread evenly around the world. Instead, they tend to be clustered in certain areas. The world's biggest reserves of conventional oil are in the Middle East, with significant deposits in Venezuela, Canada, Russia, Nigeria, and the United States. Natural gas is also centered around the Middle East and Russia, though there are significant deposits elsewhere in the world, too.

Reserves of shale gas and shale oil are found in many other places, and fracking has opened up whole new areas to oil and gas extraction. Some of the largest reserves of shale oil are in Russia, China, the United States, Argentina, Libya, and Australia. The largest reserves of shale gas are in China, Argentina, Algeria, the United States, Canada, and Mexico.

These pumpjacks are extracting oil from an oilfield in Kern County, California. About 15 billion **barrels** of oil could be extracted using hydraulic fracturing in California.

Who Fracks?

Only a small percentage of shale gas and shale oil reserves are currently being extracted. The United States was the pioneer in developing fracking technology and as of 2014, it was the only country fracking on a large scale. Other countries are beginning to experiment with fracking. China, which is the world's biggest energy user, started tapping its huge reserves of shale gas in 2012.

However, not everyone welcomes fracking. In 2011, France became the first country to ban the technique. Bulgaria joined them the following year and other European countries set up temporary bans while the safety of fracking was being researched. In 2012, Vermont became the first state to ban fracking. These bans are all motivated by fears about the safety of fracking and worries about damage to the environment.

Protests against fracking have been successful in many areas, where fracking has been either banned or strictly regulated.

FAST FORWARD

Much of the world's supply of oil is in the Middle East. Over the past century, the region's position as oil producers has made these nations very rich and given them an important voice in world affairs. The rise of fracking means they no longer have such a **monopoly** on energy production. In 2014, only 27 percent of petroleum used in the United States was imported, the lowest level since 1985. What effect do you think this might have on world politics if this trend continues in the future?

Gas vs. Coal

Fracking is opening up huge new reserves of shale gas and a lot of it is used to generate electricity. Several different types of power stations work in more or less the same way: fuel is burned to heat water, which turns into steam. The steam rises and spins a turbine, which is attached to a generator. The generator converts the spinning of the turbine into electricity.

Some power stations use coal as a fuel and others use natural gas or petroleum. In a nuclear power station, a nuclear reaction releases the energy to heat water. Although the process is more or less the same, the impact is different. Burning coal gives off more greenhouse gases than other fuels, and it causes pollution that kills thousands of people each year. Burning natural gas also releases greenhouse gases, although not as much and with less pollution. Nuclear power emits virtually no greenhouse gases, but it creates **radioactive** waste that is difficult to dispose of safely.

New regulations on air pollution mean that many coal-fired power stations in the United States will soon have to close.

The world's energy needs are constantly increasing, and fracking has played a key role in meeting those needs.

On the Way Out?

For many years, coal was the main fuel used to generate electricity in the United States and other countries. It was cheap and fairly easy to mine, and it burned well. In the early days, natural gas was considered too difficult to collect, transport, and use. However, it eventually began to be used for heating homes and fueling power stations. Today, about 30 percent of the natural gas used in the United States goes toward producing electricity.

In 1988, 60 percent of the electricity produced in the United States came from coal-fired power stations. By 2014, this was down to 39 percent, as more and more gas-fired plants were built. These modern power stations are quicker and cheaper to build, as well as more efficient to operate. They create less pollution and emit fewer greenhouse gases. In addition, fracking has meant there is much more natural gas available on the market and this has made the price of gas go down.

REWIND

In the late 1800s and early 1900s, electricity was not widely available. Many people used natural gas or other types of gas for lighting. This came with dangers, such as fire, explosion, and poisoning. So when electric lighting became available, most people switched. Ironically, much of the electricity we use today comes from burning natural gas in power stations.

The Fracking Boom

In the years since George P. Mitchell's first experiments with fracking, the technique has really taken off. The first hydrofracked gas wells cost too much to dig and fracture for the gas to be affordable. However, new technology and processes have meant that shale gas is now a huge part of the energy market in the United States.

One of Mitchell's main innovations was slickwater fracturing. In this process, a mixture of chemicals is added to the fluid that is pumped into the well. Some of the chemicals keep the well from clogging, and others reduce friction, dissolve rubble, or help the gas or oil pump faster. The exact mix of chemicals is different for each well, depending on the conditions.

The rise of fracking has been met with campaigns from environmental groups. They worry that fracking harms the environment.

Fracking technology has allowed energy companies to reach some oil and gas reserves for the first time. Back in the days of vertical drilling, reserves directly under a city or other important location could not be reached. Now, a horizontal well can start away from the source and cause less disruption on the surface.

A Fracking Explosion

Starting in about 1998, Mitchell made fracking worth the investment. A horizontal well still cost two or three times as much to dig as a vertical well, but it could produce up to 10 times as much oil. Improved technology meant that the cost of fracking was slowly decreasing. Over a 20-year period, the number of active natural gas wells in the United States doubled, reaching nearly half a million by 2009. Around 33,000 new wells are drilled each year, and more than 90 percent of them use fracking.

Those in favor of fracking argue that it will help fossil fuels last longer and reduce prices, as well as create jobs and generate money.

REWIND

George P. Mitchell died in 2013. His critics argue that his pioneering work on fracking ended up harming the environment. Some say he made it too easy to rely on fossil fuels instead of developing more sustainable alternatives. However, although fracking made Mitchell rich, he gave away hundreds of millions of dollars to charity. A lot of it has gone into research into sustainable and clean energy. What do you think is the most important part of his legacy?

Environmental Impact

There is a lot of money to be made from fracking and many energy companies now use this new technique. However, fracking has its downsides and many people are worried about its environmental impact. It has the potential to harm wildlife and habitats, as well as being a risk for human health.

Fracking involves injecting into the ground a mixture of water with chemicals. Some of the shale deposits they target are connected to underground water reserves, called **aquifers**. Accidents could lead to fracking fluids polluting these aquifers. The Environmental Protection Agency (EPA) has already ruled that several cases of groundwater pollution were caused by fracking.

Fracking uses a lot groundwater, too. Over their lifetime, some wells can use as much as 13 million gallons (49 million l) of water. One study in Texas showed that in a single year, 632 million barrels of water were used to produce just 441 million barrels of oil. Anti-fracking campaigners argue that the process uses too much water.

The danger of water pollution is one of the main problems with fracking.

After the fracking fluids have done their job, they flow back to the surface. These fluids contain minerals, chemicals, salts, and tiny solids. Disposing of them safely has become a real problem. Some wastewater is pumped into underground wells. Some has been sent to the same water-treatment plants that handle wastewater from homes and businesses. However, most of these plants are not set up to remove the types of **contamination** found in fracking fluid.

What We Do Not Know

Fracking is so new that there has not been time to conduct thorough studies on its effects. It is hard to prove, for example, that fracking has caused cases of cancer or other diseases. Scientists are trying to find links between fracking and health problems, earthquakes, and pollution, but they are still finding more questions than answers.

A group of researchers studied cows in areas where fracking takes place. Their results suggest the possibility that exposure to fracking fluids caused birth defects and death.

The Energy Future: You Choose

Some landowners have become very rich by leasing their land to fracking companies. They give permission for the company to drill on their land in return for a percentage of the profits. If you were offered a similar deal for the land your home was on, what would you do and why? Would the potential earnings outweigh the environmental impact?

Political Controversy

Fracking is a political issue as well as an environmental one. National and local governments have the power to make laws to restrict or ban fracking. Support for fracking varies between regions. The state of Vermont, for example, has completely banned it. Other areas allow it and have even offered financial incentives to fracking companies.

There are several good reasons for governments to support fracking. It can boost the economy by creating new jobs, and tax money can be raised from the sale of oil and natural gas. More fuel on the market usually means lower prices, which helps consumers. The use of fracking in the United States is seen as a way for the country to become energy independent. This means not relying on other countries to supply our fuel.

In 2014, Russia temporarily cut off gas supplies to Ukraine. Many people believe it was because of political disputes between the two countries. If Ukraine were energy independent, Russia would not have this power over its neighboring country.

However, there are also a lot of good reasons for governments to restrict fracking. Part of the job of any government is to make sure that its citizens are kept safe. They pass laws to prevent pollution and protect natural resources so that private companies cannot put people in danger. Governments also have control over huge areas of public land, along with a responsibility to preserve it.

Around the World

So far, the United States has led the world in fracking, but other countries are catching up. In many places, particularly Europe, there are strong protests against fracking. Some countries have banned it completely and others have issued temporary bans while more safety studies are conducted. Many of these countries depend on imported gas and oil and would like to be more energy independent. For example, Russia is the main supplier of natural gas to the countries of the European Union. If political disputes caused this supply to be cut off, it could have a huge impact.

Colorado has put in tougher distance requirements for fracking next to residential homes and dwellings. This image shows just how close to homes fracking was allowed to take place in Colorado.

The Energy Future: You Choose

When making decisions, politicians must balance the need for a healthy economy against concerns about health and safety. Fracking makes financial sense, but that is only part of the story. Which factors do you think should play the biggest role in a decision about whether to allow fracking in the future? Explain your reasons and support them with examples from this book.

Pros and Cons

The world's supplies of traditional natural gas and oil are being depleted, so it is important to find replacements. Engineers are still working on ways to make renewable energy such as solar or wind power cheaper and more efficient. In the meantime, fracking can help make existing oil and gas supplies last longer. However, not everyone thinks this is a good idea.

Here are a few of the main arguments supporting fracking:

- Fracking creates jobs.
- The sale of shale oil and shale gas raises tax money.
- More gas on the market means lower prices for consumers.
- Extracting shale gas and shale oil can make countries more energy independent.
- Natural gas burns more cleanly than oil or coal, so using it to replace these fuels is better for the environment.

Lower energy prices can have an effect on the things you buy. When it costs less to make and transport goods, their price often goes down.

Here are some of the arguments against fracking:

- Fracking uses a lot of water, which is needed for homes, businesses, and wildlife.
- The chemicals used in fracking can pollute water supplies and other aspects of the environment and they may cause illness or death.
- The wastewater created by fracking is difficult to dispose of safely, and pumping it underground is possibly the cause of several recent earthquakes.
- Fracking is taking away investment from other types of power that are cleaner and more sustainable, such as wind power.

More Answers Needed

Many of the concerns about fracking cannot be answered until more research is done. For example, the number of earthquakes in normally quiet areas has risen, but it is not always clear whether the fracking industry was the cause of the earthquakes. Scientific studies can take years to produce results, and in the meantime our growing energy needs create more pressure to allow fracking.

Scientists in many areas are hard at work trying to determine the exact effects fracking has on the environment.

The Energy Future: You Choose

Now that you have learned the advantages and disadvantages of fracking, you can see what a tricky issue it is. The potential benefits are huge, but so are the potential dangers. Many people support the idea of fracking, but still do not want to have a gas well near their homes. Would you support a company's proposal to frack in your local area? Why or why not? Give reasons for your answers and support them with evidence from this book.

The Future of Fracking

Like it or not, it looks like fracking is here to stay—at least for the near future. Although the industry may become more strictly regulated, it is not likely to disappear entirely. The appeal of cheaper, more plentiful supplies of gas and oil may cancel out objections to fracking. Improved technology should make it safer and cleaner.

No one can agree on exactly how much shale gas and shale oil is trapped beneath Earth's surface, but there is no question that there is a lot of it. However, some of these reserves are easier to extract than others, and many reserves may prove too expensive to tap. The EIA estimates that the United States has enough natural gas to last about 87 years. This figure could change if the amount people use increases, or if improved technology opens up new reserves.

This beautiful area in Colorado sits above a big shale gas basin. If it were opened up to fracking, it could alter the landscape.

New laws about fracking will be affected by the results of scientific studies. For example, the EPA has been studying the impact fracking has on the environment since 2011. Its study includes two locations that had not yet been fracked. This will allow them to compare results with those from areas where fracking is already taking place.

New Technologies

Many companies are researching technologies that will make fracking safer and cleaner. For example, some are experimenting with using reusable propane gel as a fracking fluid instead of water. Others are developing new ways of treating contaminated wastewater. Some engineers are trying to make cars powered by natural gas more practical. At the moment, they are much more expensive to buy, even though the fuel to run them is cheaper than gasoline.

Natural gas fueling stations may soon become a common sight as the technology for using natural gas in cars improves.

FAST FORWARD

There will likely be a gap between the time when conventional oil and gas production starts to decline and when renewable energy sources are cheap, effective, and plentiful enough to replace it. Many energy experts see fracking for shale gas as a way of bridging that gap. Would we be better off focusing our research on cleaner renewable energy sources instead of shale gas?

Power Up!

Fracking has the potential to change the world. It allows us to tap into large reserves of oil and gas. By making countries more energy independent, it could shift the balance of political power. However, it also has its dangers: unregulated fracking could lead to dangerous earthquakes, contaminated water supplies, and increased greenhouse gas emissions.

What Can You Do?

Energy policy may seem to be something for companies and governments to figure out, but you can make a difference. If you feel strongly about fracking, let your local politicians know! Public pressure has been behind many of the bans on fracking. You can also help by using less energy. If we all use less energy, then the energy we have will last longer. Think about how you can save electricity in your home, such as by turning off lights when they are not in use. Try to cut down on car travel: ride a bicycle or use public transportation instead.

Every voice matters! If you want politicians to support clean, renewable energy, you need to make your opinion heard.

Clean Energy!

Activity

Try this activity to see a model of how the rocks that contain oil and gas are formed.

You Will Need:

- A rolling pin
- Seashells
- Sand
- Pebbles
- A large clear jar with lid
- Water
- A spoon
- Leaves
- Plaster of Paris
- A foil pie pan
- A measuring cup

Instructions

1. Use the rolling pin to crush the seashells, then mix them with the sand and pebbles.
2. Put your mixture into the jar and add several cups of water.
3. Stir the mixture and watch what happens. Do the heavier materials sink to the bottom?
4. Tear the leaves. Add them to the jar, and swirl it all around. In Earth's crust, some plant matter will mix with sand and shells to form sedimentary rock.
5. Add plaster of Paris to the jar, using approximately 1 cup (235 ml) of plaster for every 5 cups (1.2 l) of the water and sand mixture. Mix thoroughly and pour it into the pie pan until it is filled halfway.
6. Leave the pie pan in a warm, dry area to dry for several days.

What Happened?

The water should **evaporate**, leaving the solid material behind to harden on the bottom of the pan. This is how sedimentary rocks are formed. Materials such as sand and other rock mix with organic material such as plant and animal remains. Then the water is squeezed out or evaporates, and the mixture hardens into rock. Sedimentary rocks often look striped, because they are laid down in layers, one on top of another.

Glossary

Please note: Some bold-faced words are defined where they appear in the text

aquifers Underground layers of rock, sand, or gravel that contain water

atmosphere The layers of gases that surround Earth

barrels Units of measure for oil; There are 42 gallons (159 l) in one barrel.

borehole A hole dug into the earth to find water, oil, or other resources

climate The normal weather conditions that an area has over a long period of time

climate change The increase in the temperature of the atmosphere near Earth's surface that can contribute to changes in global climate patterns

contamination Pollutants or poisonous substances that may harm living things

efficient Operating or working in a way that gets results with little wasted effort or materials

environment The conditions of the area where you live

evaporate Change from a liquid into a gas

explosive A substance that blows up materials

extract Remove or pull out

fossil fuels Energy sources made from the remains of plants and animals that died millions of years ago and were buried

generator A machine that changes motion into electrical energy

greenhouse gases Gases in the atmosphere that contribute to the greenhouse effect

habitats Places where a plant or animal usually lives

horizontal Straight across, rather than up and down

monopoly Complete control over a service or product

patented Covered by a legal document to make sure no one can copy it

pipeline A long line of pipes for moving gas or oil from where it is produced to where it is used or sold

pollution Materials that are introduced into the environment and cause harmful or poisonous effects

porous Having many tiny holes that allow gas or liquid to pass through

pressure The force that is produced when something presses or pushes against something else

prospectors People who search for the natural occurrence of natural gas, oil, gold, and other minerals

radioactive Giving off high-energy rays and particles

refined Made pure or into other products; Oil and gas must be refined before they can be used.

renewable Something that renews itself once it is used

reserves Supplies of something that are stored so that they can be used later

shale A type of rock made of many thin layers that can be split into sheets

sustainability Not completely using up or destroying natural resources

turbine A machine with rotating blades

vertical Up and down

wastewater Water that has been used and discarded by sewage or industrial processes

Learning More

Find out more about fracking and its effects.

Books

Bjorklund, Ruth. *The Pros and Cons of Natural Gas and Fracking* (The Economics of Energy). New York, NY: Cavendish Square Publishing, 2014.

Einspruch, Andrew. *What Is Energy?* (Discovery Education: How It Works). New York, NY: PowerKids Press, 2014.

Flounders, Anne. *Power for the Planet* (Our Green Earth). South Egremont, MA: Red Chair Press, 2014.

Nagelhout, Ryan. *Fracking* (Habitat Havoc). New York, NY: Gareth Stevens, 2014.

Websites

Find out about fracking and watch a video of the process in action at:
www.oilandgasinfo.ca/fracopedia/hydraulic-fracturing-explained

The EPA website has lots of information about fracking and its environmental impact:
www2.epa.gov/hydraulicfracturing

Watch a video explaining some of the issues and risks surrounding fracking at:
http://enginterns.com/fracking-explained-opportunity-danger

Discover the different careers available in the oil and gas industry at:
www.oilandgascareerinfo.ca/careers/career-categories

Index